I0466323

THE
CREDIT SCORE
BLUEPRINT

SIMPLE WAYS TO IMPROVE
YOUR CREDIT TODAY

BY

JEFF LEIGHTON

Important Disclaimers

Table of Contents

Author's Note

For additional resources and information including helpful videos, downloads, mentoring, online programs, and much, much more go to www.jeff-leighton.com.

Introduction

Your credit score plays a massive role in your financial life, and it is vitally important that you understand what it is, how it's calculated, and how you can achieve an amazing score. This number is calculated by the three major credit bureaus (Experian, Equifax, and Transunion) and shows how well you have managed your finances over time. Your score is essentially a financial scorecard, and the higher it is, the easier it will be for you to apply for everyday financial obligations such as a car loan, mortgage, credit cards, job applications, and more.

A good score is often equated with more trust. The more trust you have, the better the deal you will get. In this book, we will go over everything you need to know about how your score is calculated, as well as what you need to do to achieve a high score. By the end of this book, you will be an expert in credit scores and the credit industry. You will even be able to teach others if you choose to. Since this book is straight to the point without much fluff, I would recommend going through it a couple of times to internalize all the valuable information. Let's get started!

FICO Score: How It Is Calculated And A Brief History

Having a good understanding of how your FICO score is calculated will help to boost your credit score since you will know how it operates. Five main factors go into your credit score: your payment history, amounts owed, credit mix, length of credit history, and new credit.

The first part of your credit score, which makes up 35% of it, is your payment history. This is fairly straightforward. A lender wants to know how you have been in the past with repaying loans and credit since it is a good indicator of your future ability to pay. A couple of late payments here and there will not kill your credit score; however, even better would be a history of no late payments on your credit history.

Your payment history will be drawn from any credit cards you may have, any car payments, student loans, mortgage, or any retail accounts from department stores. Another big factor in payment history is any type of public record or collections that you may have had, including liens, bankruptcies, foreclosures, and any other kind of public collection. With any late payments, your FICO score will be affected by how late they were, how much was owed, how recent it was, and how many late payments you may have had. A history of late payments can bring a score down quite a bit.

The amounts you owe is the next largest factor that goes into your credit score. It accounts for 30% of your score. This is also known as your credit utilization ratio and how much of it you are currently utilizing. Owing money on any of your accounts is not bad, but what brings down your score is if you are using a high percentage of your available credit and are close to being maxed out.

The credit bureaus have determined that someone who is using a high portion of their credit is more likely to make a late payment or miss a payment. Ideally, you want a low utilization ratio, which is why it's important to pay down any debt and ask for credit limit increases with your banks or credit card companies every six months or so. You would be surprised at how many of your current credit accounts could be significantly increased just by asking for an increase from your bank or credit provider.

The next big factor that goes into your credit score is your length of credit history, which accounts for 15% of your score. The longer you have used credit, and done so responsibly, the better your score will be. Without any track record, you could look riskier as a borrower in the eyes of any potential lender. This is why you should never close old accounts because that will erase any history you had.

The mix of your credit that you currently use is the next biggest factor in your score and accounts for 10%. You will have a higher score if you have different types of credit accounts, such as a car loan, mortgage, retail account, and others. That's not to say you should go into debt and leverage yourself to obtain all these types of credit, but this is something you can responsibly obtain over the course of a year or two. Try to mix it up and use as many types of credit available.

New credit is the last factor that goes into your score and accounts for 10% of your FICO score. If you are newer to the credit game and have opened a lot of new accounts recently, this can represent a potentially higher risk to any lender.

The way to get around this is, first of all, not to open too many accounts too soon. The second thing to keep in mind is, try to avoid having too many hard inquiries into your credit in a short period of time. If you are just building your credit, you need to be patient with opening accounts and inquiries. Focus on paying on time, not utilizing too much of your credit, and building a solid foundation so that you can build your credit steadily over the course of several months or a year if you are just getting started.

Biggest Benefits Of A Good Credit Score

There are numerous benefits to having a good credit score. The first one is that you get lower interest rates. In this section, we will go over several everyday examples.

On the extreme end of things, if you have bad credit, the only people willing to lend you money or finance anything for you will fall under the category of predatory lenders with high-interest rates since it's such a risky loan. However, on the other side of things, if you have good credit, that means you will get the lowest interest rates, which will give you more money for other things.

The next benefit to a good credit score is that you are more likely to be approved for a credit card or loan. Any time you apply for a new credit card or loan of any sort, the first thing any underwriter will check is your credit score. If you already have a good, established score, you will have a much higher chance of success and approval for new credit.

Having a good credit score will also enable you to get higher limits on your existing credit. Many people with good credit don't realize they could ask their bank or credit card provider for an increase on their spending limit. Chances are, if they have good credit, they will get approved for the new limits.

I have made it my goal to get over one million in available credit, and I am getting closer to that every month. Because you have proven you are responsible with your money, the bank and credit card company will want to lend you more of it. I know some people with high credit that ask for significant increases to their credit limit every four to six months and almost always get approved.

When you apply for a new apartment or lease, part of the application is running a credit score. Having been a landlord myself, I can tell you firsthand that a bad credit score almost immediately eliminates someone as a candidate for the rental. While having a high credit score does not guarantee you will get the apartment, it plays a huge factor in your success rate.

Believe it or not, many job applications now require credit scores. While you can technically decline to give your potential employer a credit score, it is something an employer will take into consideration. Hiring managers want to consider everything these days, including your résumé, references, and credit score. Having a poor credit score could be the determining factor in whether or not you get hired for a competitive position. Especially if you are applying for a job in the financial industry, they are looking for someone who has been dependable with their finances.

Another significant benefit of having good credit is that you get better car insurance rates. Insurance companies do a ton of research and underwriting to determine the best prospects for their insurance and how much they charge. They have found that people with bad credit file more claims. As a result, the insurance companies charge them a higher insurance premium. While you can't be denied car insurances solely because of poor credit, they can still charge you a lot more. There are a couple of states that don't allow insurance companies to set prices based on credit scores, but those are few and far between. Bottom line, if you want to pay less for insurance, then you'd better get a good credit score.

When you set up the various utilities at a house or apartment, the utility companies will check your score. If you have a poor credit score, you will often have to put down a deposit, usually totaling several hundreds of dollars for each utility company. If you have a good credit score, you can avoid this altogether, and the utility companies will waive your deposit fee.

If you have a stellar credit score, you will be in a great negotiating position when it comes to anything related to your personal finance, including car loans, credit card interest rates, and more. You will have more leverage with a good credit score and receive many more offers for credit from which you can then cherry-pick the best ones. If you have low credit, you typically have to settle for whatever rates your creditors want to give you.

Lastly, you can have bragging rights with a good credit score. Put your score up on your wall and frame it if you want to remind yourself to keep your credit rating at the top. Overall, a good credit score helps you in many different areas of your life, and it is something you should feel great about.

What You Should Do If You Have No Credit Score

Getting a good credit score can be the ultimate catch-22. You need a good credit history to get any type of loan, but you can't get credit without a history of borrowing successfully. Fortunately, there are a couple of credit strategies that you can use if you have no credit and are starting from zero.

The first way, which we also cover later in the book, is to become an authorized user. If a trustworthy family member or friend (usually a parent) is willing to add you as an authorized user on their card, then that can be a very simple way of building your credit from zero. Another strategy would be to take out a small loan and have a parent, family member, or friend co-sign the loan with you. This would be much riskier for them since, if you defaulted, they would be on the hook. However, by taking out a small loan and then repaying it quickly, you can start to build credit. You can even take out the loan for the sole purpose of building your credit, which is not uncommon.

Another strategy is to apply for a secured credit card. With a secured credit card, a deposit is required, usually the amount of your limit for the card. Once you have a history of paying on time, they will extend more credit to you. However, with these secured cards, make sure you ask them and find out if they report to the three major credit bureaus. If they do, then be sure to pay your bill on time, keep your utilization rate under 20%, and verify whether they have any exorbitant fees associated with opening an account.

The next tip is to try to mix up your credit and get some type of car loan or personal loan. The more variety of credit you have, the better your score will be. Your local bank would often be willing to provide a personal loan as long as it's secured.

This can be a great way to start building credit. You can also apply for store credit cards since those are not as strict in their underwriting as other credit cards. Again, with this type of card, be sure not to use a large percentage of the available credit and pay your bill on time every month.

Once you have a track record of perfect payments with a secured card, co-signed loan, in-store credit card, or other personal loan, you are well on your way to building a solid credit score. Now it's time to apply for a major credit card, and you will have many more options once it comes to credit and loans.

SECTION 4

Get Your Scores

Getting your credit score is the first step in your journey to credit mastery. Your score can be found in several places. Nowadays, if you have a credit card, your credit score is often on your credit card statements or readily available when you log into your online banking account.

The next best place to get your score is any of the freely available sites such as CreditKarma.com, CreditSesame.com, and Credit.com that do not charge you any fees for checking your score. They make money by offering various types of financial products and services on their site, but don't worry, you do not need a credit card to get your score. Some sites out there will charge you a nominal amount to get your score and eventually start charging you a monthly fee, so be careful of those.

There are also other ways of getting your score, including buying it at myfico.com or talking to a local non-profit credit counselor. However, I would recommend using one of the free sites mentioned above. It is the easiest way, and it won't cost you a dime. You should be monitoring your score every month or so, especially if you are making any large purchases or have any major life changes in your finances.

Understanding Your Credit Score

Your credit score is the number that any potential lender will use to determine how likely it is that they will be repaid if they give you a loan or credit card. Your credit score is the credit history you have and ranges anywhere from 330 to 850. The higher your score, the less risk any lender will have, while the lower the score, the higher the likelihood that the person may miss a payment or not pay back at all.

Several factors go into your credit score, including the amount of your debt, the type of accounts you have, your history of paying on time, and the age of your credit accounts.

Lenders use this information to determine your creditworthiness and how much or whether they can extend credit to you. There are three credit bureaus that score your credit: Equifax, TransUnion, and Experian. We go more in depth on this topic later in the book, but this information should give you a general idea of what your credit score is and how it is developed.

Credit Score Myths

Within the credit industry, there is a lot of misinformation. In this chapter, we will expose the top myths that people may believe about their credit score.

1. Checking Your Credit Score Will Hurt Your Score.

This is one of the most common myths I hear, and it needs to be corrected. When you go to check your report as a consumer, it has ZERO effect on your credit score. It is called a "soft pull" on your credit score, meaning the inquiry will not be recorded on your report. If you ever have any doubts as to whether it is a soft pull, hard pull, or inquiry, you should ask. The information is readily available. Soft inquiries include things like checking your credit score online, pre-approved loan or credit card offers, and background checks from employers.

Hard inquiries to your credit are made when you apply for auto loans, student loans, business/personal loans, a mortgage, or a credit card. If you are applying for these types of loans, there is no way around getting a hard inquiry on your credit report. You just don't want too many hard inquiries within a short period of time because that can lower your score. Too many hard inquiries lower your score because it may indicate you can't qualify for the credit you need or are in some type of desperate situation for credit. Soft inquiries, however, are no factor. You can check your credit score as much as possible, at least once a year.

2. Your Three Credit Reports From The Three Credit Bureaus Should Be The Same.

In almost every scenario, your three credit scores are slightly different. The reason they are different is that different accounts are sometimes not reported to all three bureaus. Also, the credit bureaus update their ratings at different times, so sometimes they are a couple of days apart. Lastly, the credit bureaus use various credit scoring models to come up with their score and some bureaus give more weight to different parts of your score than other bureaus do.

3. Bad Credit Only Affects Your Finances, Not Your Job.

If you are applying for jobs, it is now a federal law that potential (and current) employers can use your credit score as a factor for things such as hiring and promoting. Depending on what industry or job you are applying to or currently have, maintaining a good credit score could be an essential part of the hiring process. Employers are now looking at as much information as possible for any potential candidate they bring on, including credit scores and even social media and other things. A bad credit score could indicate to a future employer that you lack responsibility.

4. Your Credit Score Affects Your Ability To Travel Internationally.

This is false. You could have the worst credit score in the world, and there would be no restrictions on your traveling eligibility. According to CNBC, about a third of consumers believe that having a high credit score is required to travel internationally.

5. You Need A Lot Of Cash In The Bank To Have Good Credit.

This is also false. The amount of cash you have in a bank does not affect your credit score. On a credit report, your bank balance or amount of assets is not listed. The only time it can be a factor is if you are bouncing checks or your balance gets turned over to a collection agency. Credit scores are based on your past performance with credit, not your future ability or cash assets.

6. Your Spouse's Credit Does Not Matter If You Have Good Credit.

Credit scores are reported on an individual basis, not on a joint basis, i.e., marriage. If you are both applying for a loan because one person could not qualify individually, then both people's scores will be looked at, not just the best score. If your spouse has a terrible score and you are both applying for a loan, it could mean you'll get higher interest rates or even be denied due to poor credit history.

7. To Boost Your Credit Score, You Should Pay Off All Your Accounts And Close Them.

This myth is only half true. One of the best ways to improve your credit score is to pay down as much debt as possible. Having high balances is one of the biggest factors that make up your credit scores. However, if you close your accounts, it will make your balances seem higher since you no longer have that previous credit limit on your balance. You should keep the credit limit open so that it shows you are only utilizing a smaller percentage of it. Also, having a credit history is something that can affect your credit score so you should almost never close an account tied to your credit. That is a big mistake, instead, keep it open and use it minimally throughout the year.

8. Your Level Of Education Affects Your Credit Score.

Education level is not something that goes into a credit report. It does not matter if you never graduated middle school or if you have an MBA from Harvard. Credit scores are only related to debt and your ability to pay it off. We have an entire section dedicated to the credit score formula, but you do not need to worry about education level when it comes to your credit score.

9. You Will Never Be Able To Get A Loan With A Bad Credit Score.

While it is harder to get a loan with a bad credit score, many companies specialize in lending to people with bad credit. The loans typically have a higher interest rate since the risk is higher. Sometimes they may also require you to have some collateral with the loan.

10. Your Credit Score Only Changes Once A Year.

Many consumers believe their credit score stays the same throughout the year or only changes once every six months. In reality, your credit score can change monthly, depending on when creditors report information to the bureaus. Make sure to stay on top of your score by checking it consistently. Some people check it once a month.

11. I Won't Be Applying For Any New Credit, So I Don't Need To Worry About My Score.

This is completely false. You should be proactively building your credit score as much as humanly possible. Having good financial habits is something you should build regardless of whether you think you may be applying for credit or not. Situations and circumstances are always changing. In fact, you would be wise to build up as much credit as possible when you are making money and don't have much debt to be proactive. Also, it takes time to build credit, so just because you don't need it tomorrow, that does not mean you should not build up your score. Additionally, there are other reasons outside of getting a loan for which you need good credit, including applying for a job or getting a good insurance rate.

12. Your Income Affects Your Score.

Many people believe the amount of income they make will determine their credit score. While having a higher income could certainly help you pay any bills or loans, your income does not affect your actual score. For example, I have a lender friend who was doing loans for several professional athletes. While they literally had million-dollar salaries, their credit scores were so low that they would have to pay cash for the majority of the loan since no lender wanted to take that risk. There are plenty of people with lower incomes who are more responsible and have higher scores than those with a higher income, and vice versa.

SECTION 7

—◆—————◆—

Tactics To Boost Your Credit Score

1. Make Sure Your Credit Score Is Accurate And Correct Any Errors.

We talk about credit repair companies in a later section of this guide, but disputing errors on your credit score can be an excellent strategy for improving your credit score. According to the FTC, around 25% of US consumers have found errors on their credit reports, so this is a strategy worth trying. Moreover, the credit score industry is surprisingly heavily biased towards the consumer.

There is a loophole that credit card repair companies often use, called Section 609 of the Fair Credit Reporting Act, which puts the burden of proof for negative items on your credit report on the credit reporting agencies. In a nutshell, you can write a dispute letter for any and all negative things on your credit report, even if they are legitimate. The credit bureaus are required to respond within 30 days, or all the disputed information from your credit report will be deleted.

Because of the short time period and the endless amount of data the bureaus have to go through to prove anything, they have a hard time doing so. In many cases, they are unable to back up the dispute. This loophole is something you should do more research on, e.g., with regards to crafting the right letter. Many consumers have success with this strategy. Later on in this guide, we will discuss the Section 609 loophole more.

2. Pay Down Debt And Try Not To Go Near Your Credit Limit

30% of your credit score is based on your credit utilization ratio. One of the fastest ways to raise your score is simple yet effective: pay down your credit card debt. A huge factor in your credit score is what percentage of your credit you are using versus how much credit you have. You do not want to be using a high percentage of your credit just because it is available, as this will lower your score. Ideally, you want to use only a small portion of the credit you have available. Most lenders like to see ratios of 30% utilization or less, and people with the best credit scores typically have much lower rates than that.

3. Raise Your Credit Limits To Help Utilization Rate.

One of the fastest ways to raise your credit score is related to the previous point about utilization ratios. If you have had your credit card or line of credit for at least three to six months, you can typically ask your bank or credit card company for an increase in your credit limit. I know some people that do this three or four times a year, as long as they are making payments every month.

Raising your credit limit will lower your credit utilization ratio and in turn increase your credit score. You will appear more financially responsible to the credit bureaus when you are not maxing out your credit. Raising your credit limit also provides more of a comfort level, knowing that if something unexpected were to happen, you could probably cover it with your new credit limit. Asking for raises to your credit limit should be a no-brainer for anybody, and I would ask your credit card company or bank today about getting an increase.

4. Get Another Credit Card

If you don't have any credit at all or you have one credit card, you should open another credit card. Make sure you don't open too many at the same time, however. Keep in the mind that one of the commonalities between people with perfect credit is that they have on average three different credit cards. You don't need to even use the card that much – or at all – if you don't want to. Getting a new credit card will add to your credit history and your credit utilization ratio. There are plenty of credit cards out there for people with minimal or bad credit as well as those with fantastic credit.

5. Don't Close Any Cards.

I mentioned this earlier, but for some reason, many people think it is a good idea to close older credit card accounts. The first reason you don't want to do this is that it will cause your available credit to drop, which means your utilization ratio will be worse off and your credit score will go down. If you are not using the card very often, just set it up for autopay on something small like a utility bill or another monthly fee. Keep in mind that a big part of your credit score is your history of using credit, so the longer you have had an account, the better.

6. Mix Up Your Credit.

If you want to raise your score, you should have a mix of credit. Instead of having one credit card, you should have several different types of credit. Again, that's not to say you need to go into any type of debt, but all the people with perfect credit will have a combination of credit cards, car loan, furniture purchase, mortgage, and any other type of installment loan. This type of variety with your credit will prove to any potential lender that you are trustworthy and financially capable.

7. Become An Authorized User.

Becoming an authorized user on someone else's credit card is a proven way to build credit quickly. When you are getting started with credit, this is an excellent strategy to use, especially if you can't qualify for a credit card on your own. Being an authorized user means that you will get your own credit card with your name on it, even though you are not legally obligated to pay the debts of that card since that is the responsibility of the primary account holder. Usually, you would ask your parents, close friends, or family members about becoming an authorized user. There has to be a high level of trust since these are financial matters and you want to make sure the person you ask practices healthy credit card habits. So long as they pay the credit bill on time and you are not utilizing a large percentage of the available credit, your credit scores should start to appear or go up.

8. Make Multiple Monthly Payments.

One credit score trick that can give your rating a boost is to pay your credit card bill bi-monthly. The reason for that is the credit card utilization ratio. Generally speaking, most credit cards report your balance and payment activity to the credit bureaus once a month.

However, the date they report your balance does not always coincide with when your payment is due. In some cases, even if you are making full payments every month, it may look like you are carrying a high balance because of the variation between the reporting date and the bill date. You can always call your credit card service number and find out when they report to the credit bureaus. Then you just pay off as much as possible before that date. Another tip is to set up mid-cycle payments, where you pay your bill down twice a month to keep your utilization ratio down. This boosts your credit score.

9. Increase The Length Of Your Credit History.

A big part of having a good credit score is the length of time you have had credit. This is why you need to be patient when building your credit. The credit bureaus will typically average the agent of your credit accounts to determine the history. Of course, it's impossible to start with a long credit history if you've never had credit, so you need to start by building a foundation with one credit card and then slowly adding other credit sources throughout the year. Remember never to close any accounts because that will hurt your history of credit.

SECTION 8

Maintaining A Perfect Score

I believe the best way to be successful in any endeavor, including getting a higher credit score, is to model the best. In this section, we go over an example of someone who has achieved perfect credit and get some pro tips from him. If you replicate his strategies, or at least most of them, there is no reason why you shouldn't be able to get a fantastic credit score. Only one percent of the US population has a perfect credit score. Believe it or not, it's easier to achieve this than you would think.

The person we talk about in this story wanted to see if he could achieve perfection in the credit world just for fun. To his credit, he began this journey with a good credit score in the mid 700s and no bankruptcies or judgments on his record.

The first step he took was reading online message boards and articles, going over every possible strategy to improve credit. Next up, he asked his credit card companies to increase the credit limit on his three credit cards as often as possible, usually every six months. They ended up tripling his credit limit, and he made sure to keep very low balances on these cards so that his utilization rate was good.

After that, he decided to mix up the type of credit he currently had and bought a car, getting a loan with a low-interest rate which he paid off within six months. To add more variety to his credit mix, he also took out a 25K personal installment loan, which he didn't even need at the time but wanted to establish more of a track record with his credit. Again, he paid this loan off in six months.

After two years of paying on time, keeping his utilization rates low, and having a variety of credit, he was able to achieve the 850 credit score, also known as a perfect score. Keep in mind, this person already had a score in the 700s and a history of credit. The longer you have had credit, the more it will help your score. He mentioned that he wasn't sure there was one thing that caused him to get the perfect credit; it was the combination of all the factors we just mentioned. In his opinion, getting perfect credit is possible for anyone who is willing to follow the steps he took and replicate his success.

Marriage And Its Effect On Credit

Fortunately – or in some cases, unfortunately – when you get married, your previous credit history has no effect on that of your partner. Credit scores are not inherited or combined; they are established separately and are only based on your previous use. Your social security number is attached to your credit score and, obviously, your social security numbers are not combined when you get married, so it has no effect.

If you decide to spend a tremendous amount on your wedding and go into a lot of debt to pay for that, then yes, your credit score will be affected, but separately between you and your partner. The only time your credit score will be affected together is if you and your partner open up a joint account. However, just getting married does not automatically add you to any accounts your partner previously had. You still have to apply or request to be added to any account, and then the credit bureaus start adding that to your credit report.

If you are both applying for a joint account and one person has excellent credit while the other person has terrible credit, that could be an issue. Both of your credit scores will play a factor in the approval process, and you could be denied or given significantly higher rates if one person has poor credit. Sometimes one spouse who has the better credit may apply by themselves to get better rates, while other times you could apply jointly, accept the higher interest rates, and then make timely payments to boost the other partner's score.

Divorce And Its Effect On Credit

Divorce does not inherently affect your credit score, but there are some indirect effects that can have an impact.

If you and your spouse have joint credit accounts, such as a mortgage and credit card, and the judge has ruled that the other spouse is supposed to pay them, then you need to make sure they are paying them. If they become vindictive and decide not to pay the bills, then your credit score will be negatively impacted if both names are on the account.

The solution is that hopefully you are still on good enough terms that they hold up their side of the agreement and make timely payments on any joint accounts. Otherwise, you will need to make the payments on any bills, regardless of the divorce agreement. You can always bring up in court at a later date that they didn't make the payments, but in the meantime, you don't want it to drag your credit score down.

There is another thing to watch out for with divorce and credit, especially if it's a messy divorce. With joint accounts, your ex-spouse could rack up debt under the account if they are an authorized user. The solution to this is that you should remove one another from all individual credit accounts as soon as you can during a divorce. This will safeguard you against any spiteful spending sprees and help keep your credit score intact.

Overall, with a divorce, you should try to keep things amicable. Either way, you need to be sure all joint bills are paid on time, regardless of whose responsibility they are, and remove your spouse's name from your accounts wherever possible.

SECTION 11

Frequently Asked Questions About Credit

1. What Is A Credit Report?

Your credit report is the history and record of your credit activity. It includes all the companies that have given you credit or loans, as well as how much they gave you and whether or not you repaid in a timely manner. Delinquencies, bankruptcies, foreclosures, and lawsuits are all items that can be found on your credit report.

2. How Do I Get Copies Of My Credit Report?

As a consumer, you are entitled to a free copy of

your credit score from each of the three national credit bureaus. You should review these regularly, at least every quarter, so that you can ensure they are accurate and there is no identity theft or unusual charges. There are many freely available credit monitoring services available online, such as Credit Karma and others.

3. What Is A Credit Score?

Your credit score is a three-digit number that is calculated from your credit history. It is a factor used by lenders to determine your ability to pay back a loan. Depending on how good your score is, a lender may approve you or reject you, and either give you a low-interest rate or a higher interest rate for less than stellar credit.

4. Does Checking My Credit Report Hurt My Credit Score?

When checking your credit report, there are soft inquiries and hard inquiries. Checking your report will not hurt your score since that is considered a soft inquiry and it is recommended to check your score and report regularly.

A hard inquiry is when a potential lender or company looks at your report to determine your creditworthiness. You do not want too many hard inquiries within a short time frame because it can signal to a potential lender that you are in desperate need of credit and, therefore, a higher risk. Too many hard inquiries in a short period of time will hurt your credit, but it is still a small factor in your credit score. The most significant factors with your credit score are payment history, the amount owed, length of credit history, types of credit used, and new credit inquiries, which make up 10% of your score.

5. What Factors Go Into My Credit Score?

We touched briefly on this in the previous paragraph. Your credit score is calculated based on the algorithm below. Your payment history makes up 35% of your score, the amount owed is 30% (also known as your credit utilization ratio), length of credit history is 15%, and new credit accounts and inquiries each make up 10%. These values are then converted into your credit score, which can range from 300 to 850. Based on the credit algorithm, the most crucial factor in your credit score is your payment history since that gives any potential lenders the best idea on how likely you are to pay back any loans or credit.

6. What Is Considered A Good Credit Score?

The credit scores range from 300 to 850. Any score above 700 is considered good. We will start at the bottom and work our way up. Scores in the 300-600 range, which accounts for about 17% of the population, are considered bad. In many cases, you will not be approved for any future credit with these types of scores or will have to pay a substantial deposit fee to obtain any credit.

Scores in the 580-670 range, which accounts for about 20% of the population, are still considered subprime, but in some cases, you can be approved for credit. Scores between 670 and 740, which accounts for about 22% of the population, are considered good. Lenders have found that less than 10% of people with these scores ever become seriously delinquent.

Scores in the 740-799 range, which accounts for about 18% of the population, are considered very good. People with these scores often get great rates from lenders. Scores in the 800-850 range, which accounts for about 20% of the population, are considered excellent. With that type of score, you often get the best rates a lender has available.

7. How Long Can Negative Items Stay On A Credit Report?

Usually, negative items such as a late payment, lien, or foreclosure stay on your report for seven years from the original delinquency date. A bankruptcy can remain for ten years from the date of filing. On the other hand, positive accounts that you are paying off consistently will stay on your account for as long as the account is open.

Positive accounts that have been closed down, such as paying off an auto loan, remain on your account for ten years from the closing date. However, also keep in mind, just because you may have had a bankruptcy or foreclosure on your record, that does not mean you can't turn around and use these strategies to get an even better score than people without that.

8. How Can I Dispute Items On My Credit Report?

It is not uncommon to find an error on your credit report. Sometimes, there will be a minor error or, in some cases, a larger one. Some common mistakes on a credit report include incorrect payment status, outdated information, identity theft, information from an ex-spouse, and more.

Fortunately, it has become significantly easier to dispute items on your credit report and get it fixed. All of the three credit bureaus, including Experian, Equifax, and Transunion, allow you to quickly and easily dispute an item online.

9. Why Do I Have Three Different Credit Scores?

It is common to have three different credit scores from the three main credit bureaus, Experian, Equifax, and TransUnion. The information collected by those three organizations is often similar but not identical. Some lenders and creditors report in different ways to the various credit bureaus. As a result, you could have three different credit scores and reports.

That is why it is important to regularly monitor your credit in case one of your scores is drastically different from another. Lenders and creditors do not always look at all three scores when making a decision about extending your credit. In some cases, they may just look at one or two of the scores.

10. How Do I Improve My Credit Score?

This guide is all about how to understand and improve your credit score. Essentially, paying your bills on time is the most significant factor. Try to keep any outstanding balances low because you don't want to be utilizing a high percentage of your credit. Reduce your debt and build up a credit history with a mixture of types of credit, including credit cards, a car loan, and even a mortgage. By paying these on time over the course of a period of time, you can significantly improve your score.

What You Need to Know About Credit Repair Companies

You have probably heard about "credit repair" and companies offering to fix your credit score for you for a fee. Chances are, you may be one of the estimated 70 million or so Americans with lousy credit (according to Credit.com). In this chapter, we go over everything you need to know about working with a credit repair company since many people are skeptical of them.

What exactly is credit repair and what will these companies do for you? A good credit repair company goes through your credit report and disputes errors on your behalf. This involves them filing a dispute on your behalf with any of the three credit bureaus in question. The dispute is usually filed online.

While filing the dispute online is something you can do for free, most consumers don't have the time or know how to go through this process correctly. These companies charge a fee for the legwork and their knowledge of the credit system. It is not uncommon to have multiple errors on a credit report, so having an expert in your corner can be very helpful.

The goal of a good credit repair company is to increase your score and make sure it is accurate, fair, and fully substantiated. A credit repair company will first pull your credit report from all three of the major credit bureaus and review each of them to look for potential errors. Once they have found any possible errors, they will then file a formal dispute for each and any of the errors with the credit bureau(s). They will work with the bureau to determine whether the item should be taken off of your report.

A good credit card repair company will remove any questionable items from your credit report. The good news for you as the consumer is that the current credit laws give much more favor to the consumer than the credit bureaus.

An interesting loophole to removing items for your credit score is that every detail in your report needs to be verifiable. That means, if you have a negative item on your report from a company that was bought out or went out of business, there is a good chance they won't be able to verify that item.

In that situation, the bureau is required to remove the item from your report. We talk more about this loophole known as the Section 609 Credit Dispute in another part of the book, but it can be a great way to remove negative information from your report. Removing false or questionable data from your credit report is one of the fastest ways to improve your credit, so it can be a significant boost to your score if you are applying for a major purchase in the near future. Credit bureaus are required to respond to any disputes within 30 days, so the time frame does not give them much time to verify which plays into your advantage.

Credit repair companies charge varying rates, some on a month-to-month charge, while others offer a flat fee. When choosing a company to work with, the biggest factor is the money-back guarantee, which is hard to find with many of these companies. However, there are several that have great reviews and offer a full money-back guarantee, including Lexington Law, The Credit People, and Sky Blue.

Many people try to do credit repair themselves, which is not a bad option if there is a simple error or two. For more complex cases, or if you just want a professional to represent you, then a credit repair company can be a great option. I would stay away from any company guaranteeing you a 100-point jump in your credit score or anything that sounds too good to be true.

Also, beware of any companies that charge a hefty upfront fee before doing any credit repair. However, there are plenty of savvy and well-respected credit repair companies, like the ones mentioned earlier, that understand the business and can give your score a nice boost. Even with a top-notch company, there is no guarantee of an increased score. However, there is often nothing to lose, especially if the company offers a money-back guarantee.

Section 609 Fair Credit Reporting Act Loophole

Fortunately, today's credit laws favor the consumer over the credit bureaus. There is a little-known loophole that can help to increase your score considerably. Section 609 of the Fair Credit Reporting Act states that "a consumer reporting agency is not required to remove accurate derogatory information from a consumer's file unless the information is outdated under section 605 or cannot be verified." In other words, if accurate derogatory information in a consumer's file cannot be verified, the reporting agency has to remove it.

This law requires the company that reports the credit events to produce proof of this negative event as well as the credit bureaus.

This rule was put in place to protect the consumer from having inaccurate information used against them; however, it gives an unfair advantage to you over the credit bureaus and creditors.

It puts the burden of proof on the original creditors as well as the bureaus, which means they have to verify the records of these negative items. If they can't prove the records, they have to remove the negative item from your credit report. In many cases, they remove accurate but negative things because they cannot be fully verified by both the creditor and the credit bureau in the allotted time.

This loophole is something you can do by yourself, but there are also reputable companies that do credit repair for you and utilize all the consumer laws to their fullest and to your benefit. Some of the aforementioned recommended companies that offer money-back guarantees include Lexington Law, The Credit People, and

Sky Blue. I suggest educating yourself as much as possible about this loophole and reading reviews from any credit repair company before utilizing one.

What Credit Bureaus Don't Want You to Know

Even though the three main credit bureaus may seem almighty and powerful, there are several things you should know as a consumer that the vast majority of people don't know.

To start with, the credit bureaus are not government agencies, even though they appear as one. They are for-profit companies that make money in a couple of different ways. They sell your credit reports to the consumer as well as to lenders, insurance companies, and other businesses that may need access to decide on offering credit.

They also sell added-on services, such as decision analytics, which gives lenders more potential data than just a credit score. Additionally, they sell marketing services to other companies based on your credit history, such as preapproved offers and other solicitations you might see in the mail. Lastly, the credit bureaus offer credit monitoring services, fraud protection, and identity theft solutions. Overall, the credit reporting industry is a multi-billion-dollar industry.

Secondly, the creditor has the burden of proof when it comes to your credit report. The Fair Credit and Reporting Act give the consumer a considerable advantage when it comes to your credit score and credit fairness. Anytime you dispute an item on your credit report, the creditor has to prove that the information is accurate and verifiable. The credit bureaus have 30 days to verify and respond to any dispute. In many cases, you can have negative information removed from your account reasonably quickly, even if it is accurate, because it can be difficult for the credit bureau to completely verify any negative information that you are disputing in such a short time window.

Lastly, it is more common than you would think for there to be errors in your report, which can result in higher interest rates or even prevent you from getting a loan or a job.

The Federal Trade Commission found that one in five consumers had errors in their report. Fortunately, it is much easier than you would think to dispute any items on your report. You can dispute an item on your report online through any of the main three credit agencies (Transunion, Equifax, Experian), as well as by sending in a letter using a sample dispute letter that you can find online. You can also use a reputable credit repair service to dispute any items for you.

Overall, you need to know that you are in charge when it comes to your credit reports and that because of the Fair Credit and Reporting Act, the consumer has a huge advantage over the credit bureaus.

What Is The Fair Credit Reporting Act?

The Fair Credit Reporting Act is a federal law that was enacted in 1970. It is designed to ensure that the three main credit bureaus (Transunion, Equifax, and Experian) gather and distribute your credit data in a fair and accurate way. It protects consumers from any misinformation with regards to credit data being used against them and has very specific guidelines on how credit reporting agencies can use and collect your information. Although it was designed primarily for the credit bureaus, it also applies to banks, credit unions, and any other businesses that could make a credit decision about you. The Fair

Credit Reporting Act or FCRA provides the consumer with a list of rights regarding their individual credit history information.

1. Some of the rights that are given to you include getting free access to your credit information from each of the three credit bureaus at least once a year.

2. Secondly, only authorized users can view what is in your credit report. This typically includes banks, landlords, insurance companies, employers, and any other business that deals with credit.

3. You also have the right to know if someone has requested your credit report over the last year and, for job-related requests, over the last two years.

4. Additionally, you have the right to dispute inaccurate information and the consumer reporting agency must look into it within 30 days. If they cannot verify the information, they have to remove it from your credit report. This is where many consumers can take advantage of the

section 609 loophole of the Fair Credit Reporting Act, which we discuss in detail in another part of the book.

5. You have the right to remove outdated negative information from your record, including late payments, foreclosures, and bankruptcies. Those typically cannot stay on your record for more than seven to 10 years.

6. You can limit unsolicited credit and insurance offers based on your credit history. This law allows you to have your name and address removed from unsolicited offers by calling (888) OPTOUT (567-8688).

7. You have the right to seek damages from violators of this act. If a consumer reporting agency or a user of your consumer reports violates the Fair Credit Reporting Act, you may be able to sue them in a state or federal court.

8. You have the right to know if the information in your credit report has been

used against you. If you are denied for credit, insurance, or employment based on your credit report, you can ask the specific reason for the rejection. The company must also give you the name, address, and phone number of the agency that furnished the information.

Also keep in mind that some states have additional state laws with regards to the Fair Credit Reporting Act, so always check with your local consumer protection agency Attorney General. There are other provisions to the Fair Credit Reporting Act, but we have covered the most important ones you need to know. It is recommended to read more about this act online.

———◆———

Credit Score Mistakes

1. Paying Bills Late.

Payment history is the most significant factor when it comes to your credit score, so you need to do everything you can to make sure your bills are paid on time. Just a couple of missed payments on a credit card, car loan, or mortgage can have a considerable effect on your score. Set up auto pay and reminders to double-check that you make any necessary payments.

2. Not Checking Your Credit Report Regularly.

Believe it or not, but many people are not even aware of their credit score or may only check it once every couple of years. You are entitled to one free report every year, and many people set up a monthly monitoring service to keep track of their score. Your bank and credit card provider should also be able to provide you with your credit score whenever you sign into your online banking account.

3. Opening Too Many Credit Cards And Accounts At Once.

With your credit score, you want to have a mixture of types of credit, such as credit cards, a line of credit, car loan, mortgage, and more. However, it is a mistake to try to apply for all of these at once. That can signal to a potential lender that you are desperate and possibly getting in over your head. Instead, open accounts slowly over time. You don't want too many inquiries on your account in a short period of time.

4. Co-Signing On A Loan.

While co-signing on a loan for another borrower does not necessarily lower your score, you do need to be careful. If that co-borrower misses a payment or stops making payments, that will affect your score, even if it was their responsibility to make payments. Just be careful about whom you co-sign a loan with. Please make sure they are responsible and double-check that they have made any necessary payments.

5. Keeping Debt Levels At A Maximum.

If you have a couple of different credit accounts, you do not want to max out or keep your debt levels too high. Debt utilization ratio makes up a large amount of your score, so while a little debt is not bad, you don't want to stretch your ratio too high.

6. Closing Old Credit Card Accounts.

This is one of the most common credit mistakes out there. Many times, someone will have a credit card they haven't used in a long time and think that it is a good idea to close it and trash it. You need to keep in mind that closing a credit card hurts your credit history since you are essentially erasing it. Closing a card will also damage your utilization ratio since you will now have a lower amount of credit to utilize. If anything, keep your card and put a utility bill or two on there to keep it active.

SECTION 17

Common Credit Scams

Credit scams are unfortunately more prevalent than ever these days, and there a couple of things you need to watch out for with these. We cover three of the most popular credit score scams in this chapter, including credit repair companies, free credit scores, and phishing scams.

One of the most common scams are with credit repair companies. There are many credit repair companies out there that promise you the world; however, I would only recommend going with any of the three we mentioned or others with lots of positive reviews.

You should be careful with any credit repair company that guarantees your score will go up

100 points or anything that sounds too good to be true. Some companies ask for an upfront fee, which is another warning sign of a potential credit repair scam. The legitimate companies will not charge you a fee until the service has been completed, and any of the companies you look at should have a money-back guarantee.

Also, any credit repair company that is looking to improve your credit by creating a new credit identity is something you should be wary of. Sometimes, the company will suggest you create a new credit identity by applying for an Employer Identification Number instead of your social security number.

If you do this, you could be breaking the law. Overall, when it comes to credit repair companies, keep it simple and use one of the three we mentioned earlier or one that comes referred from someone you know, like, and trust who has many reviews.

You have probably seen "free credit report" sites all over the internet and possibly on the news. Many of these sites allow you to check your credit report for "free," but they also sign you up for a monthly charge, often without you even knowing it.

There have been countless lawsuits against this type of practice, and many of these companies have ended up paying tens of millions of dollars in fines. However, they are still out there. You are entitled to one free annual report of your credit every 12 months from each of the credit reporting companies. The official place where you can get this for free is https://www.annualcredit report.com, a website which has been authorized by the federal law. You should avoid any site that makes you enter credit card data. Your bank or credit card company should be able to provide you with your monthly credit score when you log into your online banking account.

Credit score phishing scams are another issue that has plagued tens of thousands of people. In this scenario, you may get an email from someone impersonating one of the credit reporting agencies alerting you to a change in your account or your credit score. Usually, the email will have some urgency and want you to verify your personal account information immediately.

Once you go to the link, it will direct you to a fake but similar-looking website where you will be asked personal information, such as your social security number, credit card number, and bank account numbers. There are a couple of ways to avoid this type of scam. To start with, financial institutions and agencies will not be contacting you via email requesting personal information.

Additionally, with these types of scams, the tone of the email is usually extremely urgent, almost to the point of threatening. Lastly, if you hover your mouse over the link to the website, it will be different from the actual credit or agency website. If you think you may have already been a victim to one of these scams, you could place a fraud alert on your credit file, place extra protection on your email account with two-step verification, and file a complaint online with the Internet Crime Complaint Center, which is run by the FBI.

Conclusion

You have come to the conclusion of this book. Now that you know exactly what lenders and credit bureaus look for when calculating your score, you should know what do next. Keep tabs on your credit report at least once a year, pay down debt when you can to keep your utilization rate low, have a mixture of credit, and never miss a payment. The more you build up a history of successful payments, the higher your score will rise. Put all the knowledge from this book to good use, and keep in mind the importance of your credit score and how it can affect your life. If you take care of your credit, and it will take care of you.

About The Author

Jeff Leighton is a real estate investor, financial expert, and bestselling Amazon Author. He is passionate about helping others improve their finances and their life.

Want More Training?

Go to www.jeff-leighton.com for helpful videos, free resources, downloads, additional mentoring, online programs, and much, much more.

Other Books By The Author

Available on Amazon

Follow Jeff Leighton

Instagram.com/J_Late12
YouTube.com/JeffLeighton1
Facebook.com/JeffLeighton5